POSTWAR AMERICA

NEW FRONTIER AND GREAT SOCIETY

by Brienna Rossiter

NAVIGATOR

WWW.FOCUSREADERS.COM

Focus Readers is distributed by North Star Editions:
sales@northstareditions.com | 888-417-0195

Produced for Focus Readers by Red Line Editorial.

Content Consultant: Dr. Jeff Bloodworth, Professor of American Political History, Gannon University

Photographs ©: Dick Strobel/AP Images, cover, 1; AP Images, 4–5, 13, 17, 22, 27; Prensa Latina/AP Images, 7; Henry Burroughs/AP Images, 9; Atlanta Journal-Constitution/AP Images, 10–11; Bill Hudson/AP Images, 15; Harold Filan/AP Images, 18–19; Bettmann/Getty Images, 21; Charles Gorry/AP Images, 24–25; Red Line Editorial, 29

Library of Congress Cataloging-in-Publication Data
Names: Rossiter, Brienna, author.
Title: New Frontier and Great Society / by Brienna Rossiter.
Description: Mendota Heights, MN : Focus Readers, 2024. | Series: Postwar America | Includes bibliographical references and index. | Audience: Grades 4-6
Identifiers: LCCN 2023033157 (print) | LCCN 2023033158 (ebook) | ISBN 9798889980421 (hardcover) | ISBN 9798889980858 (paperback) | ISBN 9798889981664 (pdf) | ISBN 9798889981282 (ebook)
Subjects: LCSH: United States--History--1961-1969--Juvenile literature. | United States--Politics and government--1963-1969--Juvenile literature. | United States--Social conditions--1960-1980--Juvenile literature. | United States--Social policy--Juvenile literature.
Classification: LCC E846 .R635 2024 (print) | LCC E846 (ebook) | DDC 973.923--dc23/eng/20230814
LC record available at https://lccn.loc.gov/2023033157
LC ebook record available at https://lccn.loc.gov/2023033158

Printed in the United States of America
Mankato, MN
012024

ABOUT THE AUTHOR

Brienna Rossiter is a writer and editor who lives in Minnesota. She loves learning about history.

TABLE OF CONTENTS

THE PRESIDENT OF THE UNITED
E PLURIBUS UNUM

CHAPTER 1

NEW FRONTIER

On January 20, 1961, John F. Kennedy became president of the United States. The country was in a period of great change. The economy had boomed after World War II (1939–1945). But by 1960, it had slowed down. More than one-fifth of Americans lived in poverty.

When Kennedy became president in 1961, many Americans believed the government could improve the lives of ordinary people.

In addition, people of color still faced **discrimination**.

During his campaign, Kennedy had talked about these challenges. He was hopeful. He called the 1960s a "New Frontier." He said people could work together to build a better future.

As president, Kennedy wanted to make a series of changes. He hoped to lower taxes. He wanted to improve health care. He wanted stronger protections for **civil rights**. And he wanted to increase trade with other countries.

At first, however, problems related to the **Cold War** took up much of his focus. US leaders saw **Communism** as a threat.

In 1961, anti-Communist Cubans used US planes to bomb Cuba's air bases.

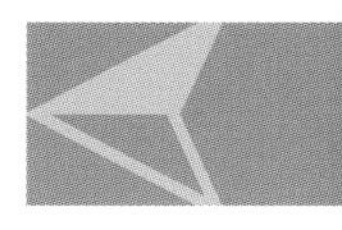

They wanted to limit its spread. In early 1961, Kennedy supported an attack on Cuba. He hoped the country's Communist government would fall. However, the attack failed. And other Communist countries, such as the Soviet Union, were angry when they learned Americans had been involved.

Tension continued to rise. In October 1962, US leaders learned nuclear missiles were in Cuba. The Soviet Union had sent them. So, Kennedy sent US ships to Cuba. He demanded the missiles be removed. Eventually, Soviet leaders agreed. But for several days, it looked like nuclear war might break out. The event became known as the Cuban Missile Crisis.

In 1963, Kennedy helped form a treaty with the United Kingdom and the Soviet Union. They agreed to limit nuclear tests to certain areas. Some testing continued. But tension with the Soviets eased.

Kennedy also helped form the Alliance for Progress. It gave aid to countries

A US ship follows a Soviet ship near Cuba in 1962.

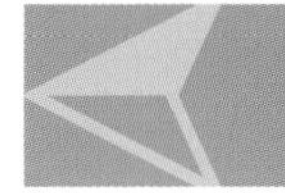

in Latin America. Kennedy hoped they would become US allies. Between 1961 and 1971, the program gave more than $10 billion. But it resulted in fewer alliances than Kennedy had hoped. Back at home, his goals for civil rights would also have mixed results.

The PRESENCE OF
SEGREGATION IS
THE ABSENCE OF
DEMOCRACY
JIM CROW
MUST GO!

The PRESENCE OF
SEGREGATION IS
THE ABSENCE OF
DEMOCRACY
JIM CROW
MUST GO!

CHAPTER 2

STRUGGLES AND CIVIL RIGHTS

Kennedy's New Frontier had many goals. One was protecting the rights of Black Americans. However, lawmakers refused to pass many of his policies. Kennedy was a Democrat. His party had control of Congress. But southern Democrats didn't like Kennedy's ideas. So, they teamed up with some

The civil rights movement took place in the 1950s and 1960s. Protesters fought for rights for Black Americans.

Republicans. They blocked many of his proposals. Kennedy did get Congress to raise the minimum wage. But lawmakers blocked his plans to lower taxes. They also wouldn't raise funding for education.

At first, Kennedy didn't press for major civil rights laws. He knew the southern Democrats wouldn't agree. Kennedy sometimes used his power to **enforce** existing laws. But in many cases, he waited until after violence broke out. One example happened in 1961. People known as Freedom Riders tried to **integrate** buses in the South. Many riders faced violent attacks. Kennedy sent US marshals to protect them. But the attacks

In 1963, a huge crowd of civil rights protesters marched on Washington, DC.

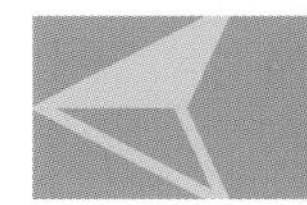

continued. So did other types of protests. People marched and called for change.

After the protests and violence, Kennedy decided to act. In June 1963, he introduced a major civil rights bill to Congress. However, he did not live to see it become law. Kennedy was shot and killed on November 22, 1963.

Lyndon B. Johnson became the new president. Johnson helped pass the Civil Rights Act of 1964. It made discrimination illegal in workplaces,

VIOLENCE IN 1963

In May 1963, activists organized a march in Birmingham, Alabama. It was a peaceful protest. But police officers attacked the marchers. They used dogs and firehoses. The event was shown on TV. It shocked and angered many Americans. Some of the marchers were children. More people began calling for change. Meanwhile, violent events continued. Civil rights leader Medgar Evers was murdered in June. And in September, a bomb at a Birmingham church killed four children.

Police dogs attack a 15-year-old protester in Birmingham, Alabama.

schools, and housing. It also gave the US government power to enforce those rules. People who didn't follow the rules couldn't get money from the government. They could also be taken to court.

ENFORCING CHANGES

Changing laws was just part of the fight for civil rights. Laws also needed to be enforced. For example, in 1954, the Supreme Court decided a case called *Brown v. Board of Education*. The decision made **segregation** illegal in public schools. But some leaders ignored the ruling. Many schools still didn't accept Black students.

In 1961, James Meredith **sued** the University of Mississippi. The school had refused to admit him. Meredith said this was illegal. In 1962, courts agreed. Even so, Mississippi's governor tried to stop Meredith.

President Kennedy sent US troops to the area. He wanted to keep Meredith safe. In a speech, he said, "Americans are free … to disagree with the

Troops help Meredith get to class in 1962.

law but not to disobey it."[1] Violent crowds fought against the troops. Two people died. Hundreds were hurt. Meredith wrote about his decision to speak up despite the dangers. He felt like he needed to act. He wrote, "If America isn't for everybody, it isn't America."[2]

1. John F. Kennedy. "Radio and television report to the nation on the situation at the University of Mississippi." *John F. Kennedy Presidential Library and Museum*. John F. Kennedy Presidential Library and Museum, 30 Sept. 1962. Web. 18 July 2023.
2. James Meredith. *Three Years in Mississippi*. Bloomington: Indiana University Press, 1966. Print. Page 219.

CHAPTER 3

GREAT SOCIETY

Johnson continued Kennedy's focus on **social welfare**. He also expanded it. He believed the government should give people more support. So, Johnson declared a War on Poverty. He helped create several new laws and programs. One was the Economic Opportunity Act. This act helped young adults get jobs and

During Kennedy's time in office, poverty rates had gone up.

training. It also gave loans to farmers and small businesses.

Johnson won the 1964 presidential election. It was a good year for Democrats. They gained 38 seats in the House of Representatives. Now they could pass laws more easily. Opposing politicians could no longer block them.

Johnson began planning many changes. In a 1965 speech, he talked about injustice and poverty. He wanted to create a country where everyone had what they needed to succeed. Johnson used the phrase "Great Society" to describe his vision. To reach this goal, Johnson urged Congress to pass laws

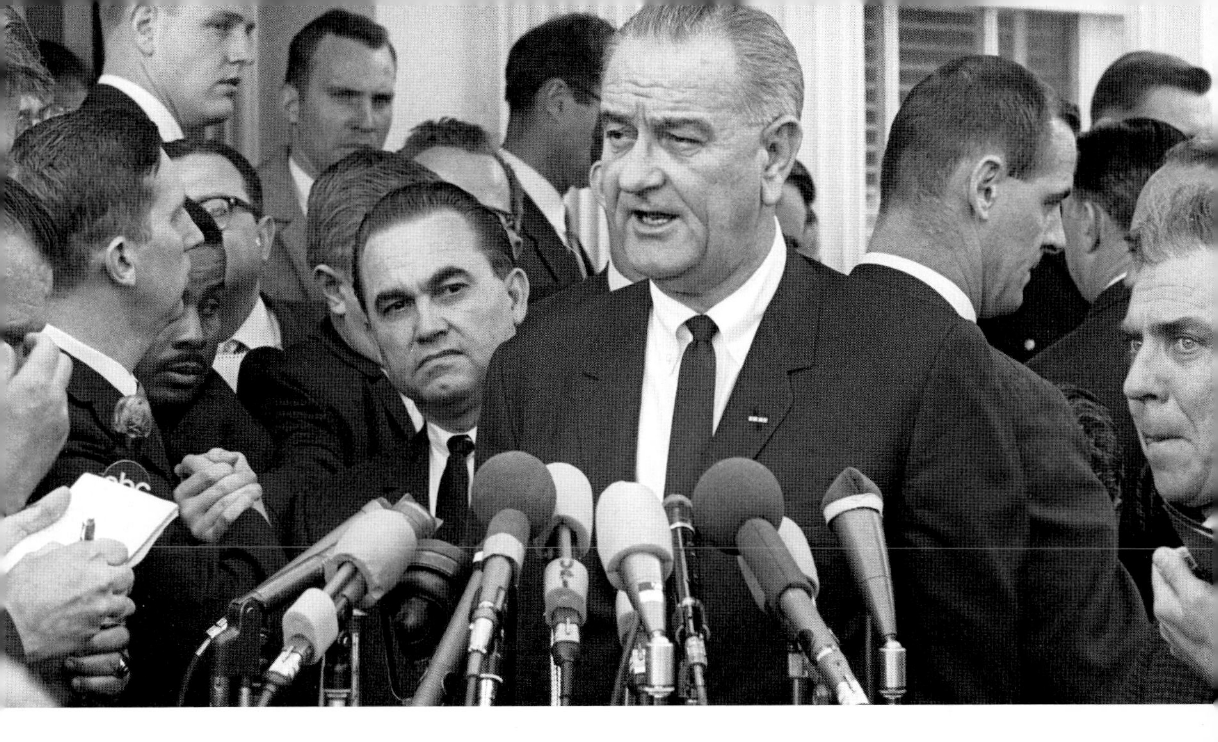

As president, Johnson worked more effectively with congressional Democrats than Kennedy did.

related to welfare. The phrase "Great Society" was used to describe those laws, too.

Over the next two years, Congress passed nearly 200 new laws. Many aimed to reduce poverty. One example was the Appalachian Regional Development Act.

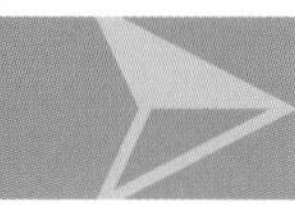
In 1965, one-third of the people in Appalachia lived in poverty.

Appalachia is a rural region in the eastern United States. The act aimed to improve jobs, education, and health care in that area. Other programs focused on cities. They provided money to build housing or pay rent.

Some laws expanded Social Security. For example, Johnson signed a law creating Medicare and Medicaid. These programs helped people pay for health care. Medicare was for the elderly. Medicaid helped low-income people.

Some Great Society laws focused on education or civil rights. All the laws aimed to improve people's lives.

EDUCATION

Education often helps people get better-paying jobs. Johnson wanted more people to have access to good education. So, he started several programs. Some gave funding to schools in low-income areas. Others offered training or funding to students and teachers. The Head Start program focused on young children. It helped meet the needs of preschoolers in low-income families.

SEAL OF THE PRESIDENT OF THE UNITED STATES

CHAPTER 4

LASTING IMPACTS

Great Society laws affected many areas of life. Several laws protected drivers and passengers. They made sure cars and highways followed safety measures. Other laws helped people get fair loans.

Immigration laws also changed. The United States had strict rules about how many people could move into the country

Johnson also signed laws related to food and toy safety during his presidency.

each year. More people could come from certain countries in Europe. However, a 1965 law changed those limits. It let more people come from other places.

Great Society laws also led to major improvements in civil rights. Activists and protesters helped prompt these changes. In March 1965, Martin Luther

NATURE FOR ALL

Many Great Society laws were related to protecting nature. The Clean Air Act and Water Quality Act were two examples. They limited pollution. The Endangered Species Act protected animals. Other laws created parks and trails. Johnson hoped to preserve the health and beauty of nature. He wanted everyone to enjoy it.

Police in Selma, Alabama, sprayed civil rights protesters with tear gas and hit them with clubs.

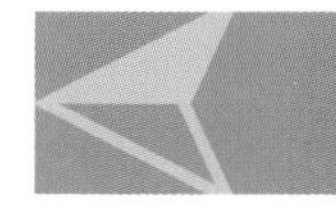

King Jr. led a peaceful march in Alabama. Police brutally attacked the protesters. The event was shown on TV. It sparked action. Congress passed the Voting Rights Act of 1965. Later, the Civil Rights Act of 1968 became law. It aimed to limit housing discrimination.

Medicaid helped many people pay for health care. Other attempts to fight poverty had mixed results. In 1964, 20 percent of Americans lived in poverty. By 1974, it was down to 12 percent. But many inequalities remained. In some places, riots broke out. A report studied the causes. It described mistreatments that Black Americans faced in society.

The Vietnam War (1954–1975) had a huge effect on Johnson's presidency. It meant he had less time to focus on social problems. It also made him unpopular. As a result, Johnson decided not to run for re-election. By 1968, his push for the Great Society was over.

Later, lawmakers ended some of the Great Society programs. Other programs are still going today. Americans continue to debate the value of social welfare.

MEDIAN INCOME

In a group of numbers, the median is the number in the middle. Half the numbers are bigger, and half are smaller.

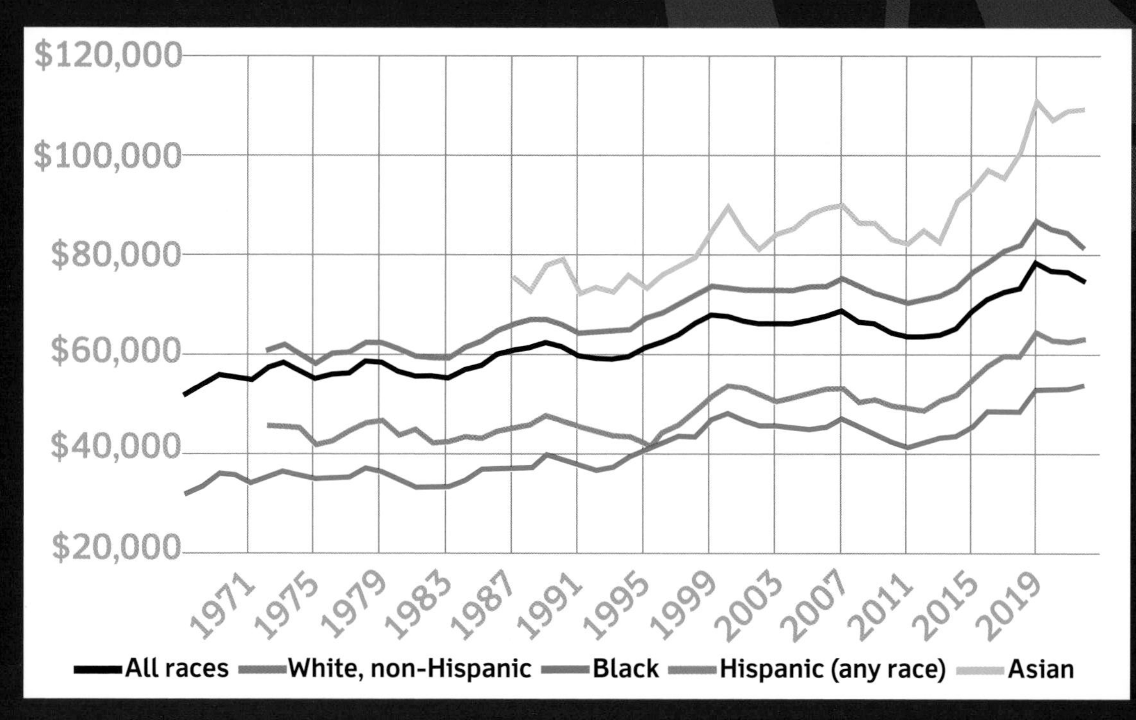

FOCUS ON

THE NEW FRONTIER AND GREAT SOCIETY

Write your answers on a separate piece of paper.

1. Write a paragraph describing some of the Great Society programs that were created to reduce poverty.
2. Do you think the government should play a large role in providing for people's needs? Why or why not?
3. Which phrase came from John F. Kennedy's campaign for president?

    A. New Frontier
    B. War on Poverty
    C. Great Society

4. How could increasing funding for schools improve education?

    A. The schools could take in fewer students.
    B. The schools could use a smaller number of buildings.
    C. The schools could pay for more workers or supplies.

Answer key on page 32.

GLOSSARY

civil rights
Rights that protect people's freedom and equality.

Cold War
A conflict of ideals between the United States and the Soviet Union that took place from 1947 to 1991.

Communism
A political idea that calls for all property to be owned by the public.

discrimination
Unfair treatment of others based on who they are or how they look.

enforce
To make sure people follow a rule.

integrate
To end a policy of segregation.

segregation
The separation of groups of people based on race or other factors.

social welfare
Programs that focus on giving help to people in need.

sued
Took legal action against a person or institution.

TO LEARN MORE

BOOKS

Gunderson, Megan M. *John F. Kennedy*. Minneapolis: Abdo Publishing, 2021.

Gunderson, Megan M. *Lyndon B. Johnson*. Minneapolis: Abdo Publishing, 2021.

Llanas, Sheila. *Children in the Civil Rights Era*. Mendota Heights, MN: Focus Readers, 2019.

NOTE TO EDUCATORS

Visit **www.focusreaders.com** to find lesson plans, activities, links, and other resources related to this title.

INDEX

Answer Key: 1. Answers will vary; **2.** Answers will vary; **3.** A; **4.** C